The Secret
Blueprint of a
Happy Life

Pooja Gupta

INDIA · SINGAPORE · MALAYSIA

Copyright © Pooja Gupta 2025
All Rights Reserved.

ISBN
Hardcase 979-8-89777-943-7
Paperback 979-8-89744-596-7

This book has been published with all efforts taken to make the material error-free after the consent of the author. However, the author and the publisher do not assume and hereby disclaim any liability to any party for any loss, damage, or disruption caused by errors or omissions, whether such errors or omissions result from negligence, accident, or any other cause.

While every effort has been made to avoid any mistake or omission, this publication is being sold on the condition and understanding that neither the author nor the publishers or printers would be liable in any manner to any person by reason of any mistake or omission in this publication or for any action taken or omitted to be taken or advice rendered or accepted on the basis of this work. For any defect in printing or binding the publishers will be liable only to replace the defective copy by another copy of this work then available.

CONTENTS

THE PURPOSE OF THIS BOOK

This book aims to shed light on the path to a happy life. Most of you understand that material gain or money does not provide true and permanent happiness. Though, material gain gives happiness as money enhances your experiences and improves the quality of life. When your attention is on ultimate goal i.e. happiness, so even if you fail in your material goals, you would not be affected and will find the way to be happy. The purpose is to be happy either with a goal or without a goal, so this book introduces few practices that can help to live life beautifully by cultivating virtues such as acknowledging your value system, perseverance, spirituality, balance perspective, etc. Hence, it's a guide to live a more fulfilling and joyful life.

Introduction of Topics

This book is an expression of life from the author's experiences and learning. This book carries significant chapters that are the pillars of success & happy life. These chapters are the author's own realizations, real-life experiences, and self-implemented practices. The author wrote this book to reveal the secrets of happiness. This book was written after vigorous study and research, inspired by many spiritual masters that resonated with the author.

If you are on the journey of living a blissful life, then come with me and join as life revolves around the following chapters from the book....

I know you are tied up with many roles and responsibilities to make a living. To accomplish these roles and responsibilities, you frequently get lost and forget to enjoy the existence of life and to be grateful for the opportunities that you have. However, each one of us deserves to live fulfilling and enriching lives.

Chapter-1

WHAT IS LIFE

Life is the process of learning, evolving, and creating meaningful moments. Life is not just about existing but about truly living—with purpose, passion, and joy.

At its core, life is shaped by your thoughts, beliefs, and actions. Every experience, whether good or bad, teaches you something valuable. Life is a blend of sadness, happiness, success and failure.

Ultimately, life is what we create. When we align our mindset, energy, and intentions, we attract abundance, happiness, and success. Every day is an opportunity to grow, to give, and to create a life we truly love.

The problem starts when you take life very seriously. According to you if you don't achieve your goals, there is no life or if you fail, life is over. The result is, that you become negative towards life. You have no hope left and you develop fear. Once you live life with such a mindset, its hindrances your progress.

The solution is understanding that any achievement in life is the source of happiness, be it a dream job, a great house, or a luxury car. In other words, if you look at it deeply, you are not looking for a dream house or luxury car rather, you look for the emotions that you get to experience after achieving it.

Fame, bank balance, status, everything takes effort. Always ask if it is worth giving your life to this one goal and get hooked-up with the idea of fulfilling that one goal. Check if it stops you to celebrate what you already have. Remember these goals or achievements are merely the sources of happiness, can we aim to be happy in small daily experiences regularly, while in the pursuit of achieving the goal.

What happiness can give you? – Happiness is the secret to achieve anything in life, you are willing to achieve. Because when you are happy, you are more productive and creative. The state of happiness will put you in the right direction to attain the desired goal because what you feel inside you attract effortlessly.

Following steps can bring happiness in your life without you waiting for a long time: –

- Spend time with yourself.
- Make other person happy in case they are important to you.
- Feed a hungry person.
- Give gifts to your workers/servants.
- Give secret gifts to someone unknown.
- Celebrate small daily experiences on a daily basis.
- Celebrate what you already have.
- Appreciate your skills and intelligence.

Here is the story of a girl who learned to celebrate life through small daily experiences. Being a Buddhist practitioner, she learned several ways to experience bliss, having an attitude of gratitude. Finding joy in others happiness. Serving and being present to others, brought her immense joy and satisfaction. This gave a feeling of contentment and, a sense of completeness. She realized that it's not necessary to be happy only after a goal has been achieved.

Keywords – Life purpose, living in the present, Perspective on life, meaning of life, Life and happiness, Overcoming negativity, True happiness, Sources of happiness, Achievements and fulfillment, Success and satisfaction, Joy in small moments, Emotional well-being.

There is no denial, that achieving a goal brings fulfillment. Since we have human body and intelligence, we want to make best use of it. We want to test our skills, grow and upgrade the level of life. While working on goals, it raises the confidence in the human being. Hence, the next chapter is about the goal setting and once you have the right goal, life is valuable and productive so let's learn about goal setting.

Chapter-2

LIFE'S GOAL

The problem is when you get confused about your goals as there can be multiple goals in your life. If you focus on one, the other one is ignored. If you pursue others, you miss out on the first. As a result, you stay confused while deciding about the goal and you feel dissatisfied in your life.

Identification of goal – For example, if the need is to get a raise in salary, then the goal should be same to achieve a better position. Once it is aligned to each other, your action will be powerful and effective.

Here is an example for you to understand the misalignment of your goal and need. When your need is to find a partner but your goal is to achieve a better position in office, now there is conflict between these two and they are not aligned to each other, hence your action will not be persistent and you will not see any result.

The other problem is following "Artificial Goal" which means you start pursuing something which is not connecting to your heart. When you fail to recognize your real value or goal and you give time and energy to an artificial goal, it results in a waste of time. For example, someone is successful in a business and you decide you will do the same. This is called artificial value. When you have the skills and its coming from your heart, is your real value.

The solution to the first problem can be dealt by following:

- Understand your needs and goals both.
- Create a sequence of needs and a list of goals.
- Check if the needs and the goals are aligned with each other.
- Check the time, money, focus and space is dedicated to your goal or to your need because wherever your time, money and focus goes you achieve that only.
- Revisit your need and goal sequence once in six months, it might change based on life's demand.
- After your need and goal is aligned to each other set the priority. Aim one at a time.

In regards to the second problem, which is identifying your real value or goal. The identification of real value can be achieved by questioning: –

- What is that one thing you love and have skills too?
- What is that, without you feel incomplete or you feel life is worthless?
- What is that one work, you think if you do, you will not be tired easily?
- What is that one thing, on which you can dedicate time easily and effortlessly?
- What is something, on which you can freely dedicate time with patience?

The answer to above mentioned questions is your real value.

Here is a story of a boy, who did 5 years of practice for football, later he realized that playing football was not his value or a goal. The guy was doing 2 hours of practice in a week and part of him didn't want to put in the hours, but he pushed himself for practice. He felt too lazy to go for practice session but soon he identified what he loves, he started polishing that and he was unstoppable.

Keywords – Artificial goals vs. real goals, wasting time on wrong goals, Avoiding misaligned goals, Success mindset, aligning life and career goals, Understanding personal values

---

After identifying a goal, what is the next thing that is very important to follow in order to achieve the goal? It will be interesting to know – what is that. Let's read next chapter to follow.

Chapter-3

PERSEVERANCE

I am sure you have small and big goals, but the problem is you give up or lose patience due to the struggle that you go through or time it takes. The goal is achieving your dream, but, because they are your dream, they are not easy.

Not being able to achieve the goal, leads to dissatisfaction and you remain dull and disappointed. As a consequence, your narrative changes towards your goal and you tend to quit.

Now the solution is to ask following questions in order to remain consistent towards your goal:

- Everyday remind yourself what it will bring to you?
- Ask how do you feel if you don't accomplish it?
- Ask yourself how do you feel, assuming you have already achieved it?
- Assume what people or family think about you once you achieve it.
- Also ask how it feels, if you don't give your best?

Let me tell you a story of a girl on perseverance who did not know how to speak English while doing her professional diploma. She was asked to read a paragraph from the Bible and daily newspapers as routine in assembly. She had no option to refuse, so she began with redness on her face, shivering hand and an uncleared voice. She could not handle the embarrassment and she was determined to hone the skill of the English language. Therefore, after one month constantly dedicating 1 hour daily, practiced unfamiliar words from English newspapers she became proficient in reading the newspaper, in front of everyone. She began to enjoy reading newspaper. Her perseverance enabled her to achieve confidence and gain respect and recognition in the assembly.

Keywords – Never give up, keep pushing forward, overcoming obstacles, Resilience in tough times, Staying committed, Mental toughness, staying motivated, Pushing through struggles, Long-term commitment, Turning failure into success, Growth mindset

---

After covering goals and perseverance. Now it is important to learn how to deal with difficult situations in life. It is going to be very interesting and full of insight.

Chapter-4

NAVIGATING THROUGH CHALLENGING SITUATIONS

The problem occurs when unforeseen situations come into your life, and it creates panic within you. As a consequence, you lose balance and you don't know how to deal with it. Actually, the situation in life comes to make you, not to break you.

The solution to be balanced in any situation can be achieved by asking the following questions –

- What can you do in this situation?
- How an optimistic person would deal with this situation?
- Think, what if you have asked for this situation?
- Why would you ask for it? What does it allow you to do?
- What opportunity it may bring to you?

Let me tell you a story of a girl who went jobless suddenly and unexpectedly, despite being excellent in her career. The day she was asked to resign, shocked her but then, after consideration, she thanked that she was out of that rut and it was time to discover a new career. She asked, what I would love to do if not in that job.

Her inner voice said, do the work which can bring change in her life and in the life of others. Hence, based on skill set and intent, she decided to enter into the training industry. She started preparing herself to be a coach. As she appreciated rather than complaining for losing a job; it brought her two options to choose from. One is to pursue entrepreneurship and coaching career. Secondly, to pursue a life of a foreign country.

While she prepared herself to be trainer, she learned science of NLP which gave her astonishing results, hence she thought to share with others so she decided to face camera and teach same on YouTube. Due to that she was able to reconnect to society for a good cause. People started sharing their inner feelings and emotions with her.

In the midst of all, the other manifestation has happened to her, is to be in the project and go to Chandigarh. Not only this one project, but many people approached her to work. She understood all of this was happening to her, because she was not impacted by the challenges. She remained optimistic and took definitive action. As per law of energy she practiced high frequency, acknowledged and celebrated life which brought end number of opportunities.

Keywords – Overcoming obstacles, Life's unpredictable moments, Facing the unknown, staying calm under pressure, Emotional balance, Strength in adversity, Developing resilience, Adaptability in tough times

---

It is true that she had aspiration to grow and learn, but it is crucial not to have impulsiveness, because the more desperate you are for something, it pushes itself far from you. It's the law of pull and push. The more you push something; more it will pull back from you. Therefore, what comes next is the power of surrender, and how you can apply, lets learn more about it.

Chapter-5

SURRENDER

The problem starts when you want to control the results and want to have guaranteed results. Anytime you start taking action, it may take time more than you expect. The faith and consistency in your actions bring the results. In case you fail to surrender and keep wondering about results and begin to question when will it happened, leads you to stop taking action and not taking action will lead to no progress. And you remain stuck in your life, nothing moves.

The solution to the problem is when you take action but you don't get attached to the results.

- Believe in every action and it has some reaction.
- Enjoy the process.
- Remember you are a doer and the universe is the giver.
- Believe the best will happen for you.

Here is a story of a girl who applied the law of surrender. A girl had a deep desire to go abroad but at some point, after enough trials & tribulation, she accepted and became easy with the idea of not going abroad. She became neutral and began to focus on Plan B. While she was working on plan b, in a short span of time, got a chance to go to another country that was not her preference, yet she gave due consideration, thinking it may be fruitful.

She completed all the procedures but had no attachment for the results because she was in a state of acceptance to any outcome. She had some savings which she utilized for this process. The process was very tedious, so doing it with no expectations was difficult because, time and money were being used. She appeared for language tests, which was online due to a lockdown. Due to some interruption in the online English efficiency Test, she felt the result would not be favorable and had no intention to repeat either, however, she was not worried about it. She remained balanced and in surrender mode.

To her surprise, she got the result with a great score. Now, it was a universal signal to her that it was going to materialize. The English language proficiency test score was well accepted by college and university in Dublin.

After getting the admission letter from college. One of her friends who does visas for students, doubted about her student visa because of a gap in studies. She mentioned that she was ready to take a chance. To her surprise, she received a visa 10 days after submission of documents, beside the error was made and the college fee was paid by using a credit card which is a negative point as per immigration.

Keyword – Letting go of control, releasing expectations, Surrendering to the process, Fear of uncertainty, Trusting the journey, Trust the timing of life, Faith in the process, Patience and perseverance, The power of consistency, Progress over perfection, Staying committed to goals, Small steps-big success, Aligning with the universe, Allowing success to flow, Detachment from outcome.

The story of this girl tells that when desperation shifts and no attachment is left, the best appears.

Practice of surrender made many goals possible to her, as she practiced the Law of Attraction in a correct way. Let's understand how this law works, so that you can make the best use of it. Law of attraction is working all the time; hence it is great to learn and practice perfectly to receive benefits.

Chapter-6

LAW OF ATTRACTION

The problem is, that people consider the "Law of Attraction" is to repeat statements and keep affirming, or staying positive. As a result, **manifestation fails and you question, if it works?** I am sure you must be feeling the same when you experience failure.

Another reason that the law of attraction does not work for you, **could be due to a lack of clarity about what you want, which creates confusion in the universe. As a result, the manifestation fails or takes time.**

To get the fastest result, let's first understand how the law of attraction works.

- Law of attraction works based on law of energy. You attract based on what you feel, or emotionalize because you emanate the same.
- The universe does not understand the words that you say, but it understands the energy that you carry within you, and it sends you the same.
- Everything in this world is energy and you are energy too, you attract the same energy based on what you are, so if you feel rich you become rich, if you feel sad, you witness more such situation. Universe gives based on what you feel inside.

Let's understand it, through a story.

A girl who didn't know about the law of attraction years back. One day she was travelling to her office, she saw a smartwatch on her phone; admired the look and said, "I love it and I would like to get one". Surprisingly, someone handed her a gift box, of a smartwatch the same evening. That left her in amazement. She could not believe it. Later she was able to connect the dots that the law of attraction is always working whether you notice it or not.

Her second big manifestation happened during lockdown when everyone's life was confined behind the walls. **She visualized a place surrounded by greenery and saw herself living there, going for morning walks etc. Out of nowhere, she got a chance to work on one of the projects, and everything from stay to travel got arranged during the lockdown.** The living place was full of greenery with a park to walk in front of the house. After that, she had many such stories.

Another big manifestation was to be in a foreign country, which got materialized in 6 months of time during lockdown.

Here is a daily practice guide from the Law of Attraction for you. Follow the step-by-step guide to manifest your desires.

Law of Attraction
Gratitude (Activity No-1)

The problem is, you offer gratitude as a ritual, but you don't live in gratitude or you don't feel grateful emotionally. As a result, subconsciously you are still in lack, which brings similar situations in your life. If you practice gratefulness at emotion level too, you create high frequency hence your energy changes and higher state brings you what you desire.

Activity of Gratitude – Practice following exercise. It is to write and read from your notebook daily.

Thank you for the health I have.

Thank for the money I have.

Thank you for the job I have.

Thank you, for blessing me with good friends.

Thank you for the family I have.

Thank you for blessing me with cloths, food & house.

Thank you, the skills and wisdom, that I have.

Thank you for the dreams I have.

Thank you for the opportunity I have.

Thank you for the clarity that I have.

Thank you for giving beautiful experience of life.

Thank you, all the blessing, that I have.

Let me share a story of a girl who did gratitude for everything. She made a gratitude general and practiced regularly. She appreciated everything she had such as good health, a good job, a house, family, friends & food etc. She practiced gratitude daily to keep her energy high. Along with a gratitude journal, she also did gratitude meditation. For example, once she accepted a job from a company on a very low pay scale, compared to what she wished for, and kept her focus on whatever has achieved and always admired that she got a family visa that resulted her family being around her due to the job.

She blessed her boss and the company after joining. She began to work with a grateful attitude and thanked her boss and universe for processing the work permit in advance. She joined as part time worker but in her mind, she manifested the family visa which has happened in reality later.

She manifested many things due to the synchronicity between her emotions and the universe. She thanked as she already had it, it kept her energy level high.

After gratitude practice next comes visualization which can immediately infuse positive energy in you. It's magical as it creates happy emotions instantly.

Law of Attraction
Visualization (Activity No-2)

Visualization is significant practice; it's a simple and effective practice to manifest. The problem is, if you don't believe in the science and you don't practice well you don't see the results. Take all possible action that you can, in your capacity as per your logical brain but also use the magic of visualization and be creative. Create it into invisible world first.

Let's learn about it how it works?

- Sit in a place, choose one place if you can, even the time to visualization is recommended to be the same.
- Imagine and visualize what you want to live and experience.
- Be in the celebration mode as it has already happened to you.
- See it, experience it and feel it now.
- Practice it daily and 2-3 times a day.

The science behind it, is the images of the experience you create during visualization get installed into your subconscious brain. Because your subconscious mind is connected with the universe, the message goes to the universe and it creates the situations to turn into reality.

Here is a story of a girl, who visualized riding a bike whenever she sat for manifestation meditation. It took her 2 minutes every round, visualizing only the end result, not the process. The process is not important in manifestation. As a result after reaching to Dublin at very early stage, she manifested e-bike to ride for day-to-day life, which ended the transportation related struggle in her life.

Now let's understand another practice of law of attraction which is walking-talking affirmation. Now the question is about how affirmation can help and contribute to your life? So lets learn about it now.

Law of Attraction
Affirmation & Afformation (Activity No-3)

Affirmation means being decisive about what you want. Keep affirming during the day, as many times as you can. This is called walking talking affirmation. Affirmation is thanking to the universe for having the results in advance and emotionalizing as if you have it now.

The problem is when you affirm, but part of you does not accept, it rejects the idea of having the feeling in advance. Since you are not able to generate the emotions of having it, hence the results are different from your expectations.

The solution to the first problem is, that part of you rejects accepting that you have it in advance; this can be handled by practicing afformation. What is afformation, let's understand it. Afformation is asking a question in your mind, why do you want to achieve this goal?

Once you get clarity by asking the question for e.g. why you want it and the answer to it –is called afformation. It allows your brain to accept the idea of having it in advance.

Following are few daily affirmations: – (the one you want to manifest) its bit different from gratitude. (Gratitude is thanking to what you have it already).

Thank you for the health I have.
I exercise daily 20 minutes.
Thank you for ideal body weight.
Thank you for the money I have.
I learn to double my income on daily basis.

Thank you for financial abundance.
Thank you for beautiful relationship with everyone.
I respect and value everyone.
I have great relationship with everyone.
Thank you for the job I have.
I give 100% in my workplace.
I receive love, respect, value and money in my work place.

Here is a story of a girl, who practiced affirmation by linking the concept of afformation after learning it from one of the coaches.

For example, she asked a question before creating an affirmation such as **"Why does she has more than enough money"**. The answer to it came because **she wanted to help others. She wants to have a sense of security**, and **she wants to experience pleasure and a rich life**.

This way, it created new images in her subconscious brain, and the conscious brain could easily accept it, because that is the truth for her.

To practice, "afformation" your affirmation which has to have why question, so first create question with why, then find the answer. Then practice affirmation.

Testimony

A girl practiced afformation to attract the stay in abroad. She asked the question – why does she wanted to go abroad, the answer to it came, because she wanted to experience different life, wanted to help others, wanted to have savings. Wanted to give a good life to her child, and wanted to live in a beautiful house, happily. After asking the question it became clear to her mind. She affirmed "Thank you for giving experience of foreign land", "thank you for giving a feeling of prosperity", and "Thank you for some savings". Whatever she has affirmed has come true to her.

This not only resulted her to be in abroad but also made her strong as a person.

Keywords – Clarity in manifestation, Defining desires clearly, Manifestation and focus, aligning thoughts and actions, Fast manifestation techniques, How the Law of Attraction works, Manifestation secrets, Energy alignment for success, Power of clear intentions, Energy blocks in manifestation, Vibration frequency and attraction, Creating the right mindset, fastest way to manifest, how to manifest correctly, Law of Attraction proven methods, Achieve desires effortlessly.

For attracting anything in life one important aspect is, to heal yourself. Heal your past memories, heal all your negative emotions, once you heal and become new, the space is created to attract new in life. When human mind is filled with negative emotions it is difficult to invite abundance in your life or anything good. Hence lets learn how to heal yourself.

Law of Attraction
Heal Your Emotions to Invite Abundance
(Activity No-4)

The problem is when you doubt healing or lack faith to heal yourself. Logical brain stops you believing. As a result, you don't give it a try and live with physical and emotion pain. Have you ever thought, before medicine was introduced to us how people used to receive healing? Whereas healing is very simple practice. It works on your aura. The moment you acknowledge the emotion that you go through or you feel, gets dissolve and healing happens.

One of the healing practice is **Ho'Oponopono** wherein, you use **4 statement – I am sorry, please forgive me, thank you and I love you.**

You use the statement **"I am sorry"** to heal what you are feeling. You say "I am sorry" because you have created the emotion, You say sorry because you are still holding it inside. You are sorry to yourself, because you are feeling helpless.

Second statement-please forgive me because you are not aware what is the lesson for you. You are asking forgiveness because you had to go through this phase. You asking forgiveness because you could not experience happy emotion. You are asking forgiveness because you caused suffering to yourself.

3rd **Statement-thank you,** for healing, thank you for cleaning which does not serve you, thank you for releasing the negative emotion from you.

4th **statement "I love you"** for making me new person, I love you for giving me what I need, I love you for being present to me, I love you for learning whatever is there in this process.

What all you can heal: You can heal the relationship, you can heal situation, you can heal the process, you can heal emotions. The process remain same to heal everything you go through.

Real Life Experience of Healing

After learning about it the girl has practiced Ho'oponopono on regular basis.

She learned first time about the healing in the year 2022, and kept exploring from other's experiences. After completing a healing certification, she practice it more religiously, because now she heard the power of it more closely. The results were magical.

She kept chanting these 4 lines. **4 months have passed and one day in the morning she questioned, when will she personally experience the magic of healing?** She became quite for few minutes then she noticed having butter form past one month in diet. Surprising it didn't show any allergy. She had no pain in her stomach. It was new to her, because she could not eat any oily or buttery food from the age of 8 or 10. **She suffered and stopped all greasy food since childhood. It was to an extend that even in wedding she ate salad or curd, or dal and rice. She was delighted and surprised, so went to check with some more experiments. Tried oily food during the lunch.** She was alright, then she informed her mother and other family members that she is cured with that problem.

Since the Law of attraction is based on Neuro Linguistic Programming, NLP has another interesting practice. Hence, it's important to learn NLP, Are you ready to learn which is next practice?

Law of Attraction
Switch Words (Activity No-5)

The problem is when some negative situation comes, you get carried away by it, sometimes for hours, days or even weeks. As a result, it infuses negative energy into the body which takes you away from manifestation. To handle, any negative situation, the best way to counter it and generate some positive emotions. Switch words are an instant dose to remove negative emotions and thoughts.

Let me tell you the power of it through a story. A girl got introduced to Switch Word through NLP class. She used switch words in the situation of searching something and not able to find made her worried. In this situation she used switch words like "Divine Reach Now" to find the lost stuff quickly. She realized, chanting changes the emotional state which gave her hope and put her in a positive state, as a result, she could find things easily.

Similarly, another switch word she tried for raising money frequency whenever she felt a lack of funds, chanted "Divine count Now". She found money on the road many times, and stuck money came to her. Fundamentally, what it does actually, it stops the flow of negative energy in you and bring you more of what you are chanting.

Practice following Switch words; –

Divine count now – for money
Divine order now – for good health
Diving Reach now – to find something

Diving finds on – for opportunity
Divine short cut now – to reach somewhere on time
Divine Gold On – new opportunity

Keyword-Power of emotional resilience, staying positive in tough times, Switch Words, NLP, Mindfulness and manifestation, Training the mind for success, Emotional control for manifestation.

After going through about law of attraction practices, now its time to identify your money energy.

Chapter-7

MONEY ENERGY

The problem is you think money belongs to rich people or it is for rich people only. Your vibration and your energy is reaching to money, as money is also energy. As a result, money does not come into your life easily, because as per your belief it belongs to rich people. For example, if you say continuously to a friend, that you are not my friend, will that friend be happy and would like to be with you? Will that friend become your best friend ever?

- The solution to attract money in life easily and freely, is to understand what money is first.
- You tend to create blockages for money by having a wrong belief system such as money is not easy, money spoils people, or you are not that lucky etc.
- It is imperative to have positive thoughts about money if you desire to have more in your life.
- If you believe you are worthy to be rich and have the skills to be rich, you are that, it's just yet to witness this reality in your external environment.

Here is a story of a girl who practiced, the science of money energy. She began to praise the money and began to spent with positive energy. When she spent, gave a thought that this money is going to add happiness to other people's lives.

The year 2023 she visited India and her flat was in a mess as it had been closed since 2021. It had dampness on the walls that caused damage, so the walls had to undergo repair and maintenance. She had to spend the time and money, which took a while to get it in order. The problems persisted related to electricians, plumbers, carpenters, etc. In a normal scenario, she would have felt upset and kept counting the expenses but as she practiced wealth consciousness, she could infuse positive energy into herself. She felt as if she brought work to so many people and she was blessed with money to get the job done in-house. She thanked money every day she spent.

Practice Assignment

Here is an assignment for you, print and place following affirmation in-front of you:

Affirm positive about money to raise your money frequency and invite abundance into your life.

- It's easy to make money.
- Money is my best friend.
- Money loves me and I love money.
- Money comes to me consistently from multiple sources.
- Money comes to me day and night happily and effortlessly.
- I love and respect money.
- Money loves to be with me.
- Money stays with me always
- I have best money management skills.
- My money makes more money.

Afformation for money energy, which helps practicing the affirmation:

- Ask yourself how your life will be if money is in overflow.
- What will be your thoughts if money is in overflow?
- Ask why you can have an overflow of money.
- What thoughts people will have about you, due to the overflow of money in your life?
- List why you deserve an overflow of money.
- Why do you love having so much money?

E.g. answers – you love money because you love security, you love experiencing new and rich life.

- Why are you a money magnet?

Example Answer – because people love you, people trust you, and you have skills. You can solve people's problems. People look for your support.

These practices will shift your energy. Affirmations are recommended to practice at least 5 days a week. Once written, read it with emotions.

Last, but not the least, another recommended practice is, **to make a list of your wildest dream**. While you are writing **do not use logic**. Don't limit yourself by thinking what can be achieved or what cannot be. Write everything you want to experience. Consider once you write and acknowledge, they will be fulfilled, few in this life time and other may come true in the next life. So writing the dream is fun. Once you finish writing, read it out. You will feel association & connection. Your frequency will go up.

Note – Read it with fun but no attachment. Achieving list or any other desire in life to be considered a quality time pass.

Keywords-Wealth manifestation techniques, Money magnet mindset, financial abundance secrets, Power of gratitude in wealth, attracting prosperity effortlessly, Breaking money myths, removing financial fears, Healing money wounds, releasing scarcity mindset, shifting from lack to abundance, treating money with respect, Wealth and emotional connection, Attracting money effortlessly, Positive money habits, Money and self-worth

About money, another truth is **"give what you want to receive"**. Happy money energy is created by contribution, so now let's learn what contribution can bring in your life.

Chapter-8

FINANCIAL CONTRIBUTION

The problem is stinginess about money, or thoughts of not having enough. As a result, the emotion of lack stops you from contributing. The negative emotion for money keeps you in scarcity. If you feel lack of money, it is a negative emotion hence you are ordering same emotion more. As you are not able to contribute, there is no space created for new money. Remember, what you give more, you receive more. Giving is important for receiving.

Recommended practice for financial contribution that you can make?

- It is recommended to make a 5% contribution from your monthly earnings.
- You can sometimes make a secret contribution to bring happiness in someone's life.
- If you are not making any money contribution, it can be done by offering some services and support. This practice will raise your frequency.

Here is a story of a girl, who learned to contribute in others life. The thought of contribution was infused through Buddhism in her life. Financial contribution didn't feel easy to her in the beginning. Her contribution began by chanting for others. It brought her happiness because she has the intention of giving. She learned that her small contribution can be big for someone else.

Testimony - Financial Contribution

Her financial contribution began gradually and here is one example from her life during the process of her work permit (stamp 1) where she agreed to pay a 50% fee to process sponsorship. As per the discussion, the company was supposed to adjust it from her salary. Not being aware, the lawyer has sent the invoice for visa processing to her employer directly. On the other hand, this girl made a 20% contribution in advance, listening to the podcast on contribution "give what you wish to receive", she just intended full sponsor fee is taken care by the company happily. She trusted the process and surrendered as if it was done.

Six months passed when she noticed, no deduction has happened yet. To be certain, she reminded about the communication regarding deduction. She was brought to her notice that it's funded by the employer.

She learned and experienced what you want for yourself – give it to others first. She practiced contribution and noticed a lot of support was being extended to her when needed in her life.

Keywords – Fear of not having enough, Scarcity vs. abundance mindset, Money resistance, limiting beliefs about money, Emotional blocks in wealth, Power of giving, Wealth and contribution, Money circulation, Giving and receiving, Abundance through generosity, Money is energy, Law of attraction and money, manifesting financial abundance, Prosperity consciousness, Positive relationship with money, financial flow and gratitude, Receiving abundance effortlessly.

In the process of offering prayer and you want your prayer to be answered, one thing is very important, keep your prayer when you are thoughtless. Hence, meditation is something you learn next now, to reach to the thoughtless stage.

Chapter-9

POWER OF DAILY MEDITATION

The problem is when you think mediation is meant for certain age group people only, or it is to be practiced when you are retired or free from all responsibility. Hence you end up spending important years of your life without meditating. As a result, all your life you navigate through fear and insecurity, lack of clarity in mind, and impulsiveness. The day you realize, meditation is important part of your life; by the time, significant years of your life have passed, and you end up saying –

"Wish I would have practiced it earlier in my life".

Meditation is not prescribed to certain age groups, but it's for people of ALL ages. It is important to be with yourself, know yourself and be present to your senses. Meditation helps to live life more beautifully and connect to your core, ignites the hidden virtues. You can access and see things differently, which is absent, when your logical brain is active.

Please follow the simple steps to meditate:

- Sit straight, close your eyes, and bring your attention to your breath.
- Observe every inhale and exhale,

- You will notice the breath starts from the bottom of spine (root chakra) to crown chakra.
- Visualize the energy going upward towards crown chakra with every inhale and during exhales and it returns to bottom (Muladhar/Root Chakra)
- Keep your focus on your breath, you will reach a clear mind stage.
- Achieving a clear mind or a stage of 0 is, when you are one with the universe.
- This is the time when you can manifest or keep your wish because you are in the world of creation.

Here is a story of a girl, who believed in meditation. The journey of her faith began with small achievements. Her faith got tested when she left India without her daughter, due to studies in abroad. She aimed to create a better world for her child, but not at the cost of depression and agony.

She decided to bring her daughter from India, during her unfinished study, despite friends and family's disagreement. According to friends and family, it was a fruitless effort as she was still on a student visa so she can not invite her family. However, she followed her intuition and trusted the process and practiced the law of attraction.

She kept her mind clear from all the negative emotions and energy. She knew that good intentions are always responded to by the universe. She prepared herself for any result, with a Plan B in the mind. Plan B is to return to India, in case a visa is not granted for the family. Her fear got dissolved substantially because she knew what she had to do if visa fails, she just prayed for best to happen.

She and her friend Ish chanted consecutively for a successful visa process as they believed in the power of group prayer. Her friend Ish has always been with her in her ups and downs of life. As planned, she prayed her daughter to reach before the upcoming festival. It felt miraculous as she chanted on the 24th Morning of September for a visa to stamp, and by the 25th – 26th of September, she got the news that it was under process. Within 2 days, the passport was delivered with visa stamped, and the ticket was booked. The family reached on 2nd of Oct a day before festival.

Keywords – Who can meditate? Meditation for all ages, Breaking meditation stereotypes, Meditation is not just for the elderly, overcoming fear and insecurity, Emotional balance through meditation, Meditation for inner peace, Early meditation benefits, avoiding stress and anxiety early, Unlocking full potential through meditation, Meditation and manifestation, Vibrational alignment through meditation, Energy work and mindfulness, Meditation for success.

As human beings we have some emotional ties and due to which stress is formed. Stress management seems difficult to most people, so let's learn how to manage stress next.

Chapter-10

STRESS MANAGEMENT

The problem is, you think stress is normal and it is in everyone's life. It is not true. A person who laughs stays happy, is productive and manages stress well. People who don't know how to manage a stressful situation lead to dullness, depression, anxiety etc., as a result, it causes health issues and conflicts in relationships and other areas of your life.

Here is how the stress can be handled by applying the following filters in any situation.

Filter-1. "Circle of Concern" **& Filter 2.** "Circle of Control".

Circle of Control – Is linked to you, and you can do something about the situation. However, if you are unable to do anything due to lack of courage or you fear from taking action, then it creates stress as it falls under the circle of control.

Circle of Concern – When you can't do anything in a given situation, but you stress as something occurs in a close family. Since, you are not able to do anything, hence there is no use in being stressed, and it falls under the circle of concern.

- Above are two filters which can be used in the given situation of stress.
- Always check about the given situation if that falls under the circle of control or concern?

- Every single time you stress, ask if it falls under the circle of control or the circle of concern. It means to check, can you do something about it or not?
- This activity will impact your brain tremendously, and the unnecessary stress will dissolve, if the situation does not fall under the circle of control.
- If you understand it's in your circle of control, your wisdom and gut will guide you to take the right action.
- After asking the question and realizing it's just concern, thoughts creating stress will vanish. The concern is merely an emotion of sympathy for loved ones.

Here is a story of a girl who learned about stress management during her career. It helped her to question and apply the right filter in every situation. She became bound to follow the formula of stress management, because of the knowledge about chemicals in the human body, which get released in the state of happiness and sadness. She became attentive and careful to react to particular situations. Happy hormone – chemicals are serotonin, oxytocin, endorphins and dopamine, get released when a person is happy. It is good for your health. However, the release of the amygdala in the body is caused by fear, anxiety, unworthiness harms you.

Here is an example of handling a situation – A girl undergoes a situation in her career where she felt not respected and that impacted her emotional state. She did this exercise in her mind. Asked the question if this situation is under the circle of control or concern. After realizing that it's under the circle of control, she decided to take action. She met the CEO to discuss the matter. She was asked if she could handle it at her end, second if she was taking it in a big way. She realized this discussion gave her relief because she took the action.

Keywords – Managing stress effectively, Stress relief techniques, overcoming stress, Healthy stress management, Stress-free living, Mental clarity, Emotional balance, preventing anxiety and depression, Emotional resilience, coping with life's challenge, Staying happy and healthy, Positive mindset, Stress and health issues, Healing through emotional well-being.

A lot of time stress is self-created by overthinking about the situation or by judging it. The judgement makes humans impure and bring negative energy inside. So, it is important to learn about it and practice not to be judgmental. Let's learn about it now.

Chapter-11

Non-Judgemental

The problem starts or gets created based on the judgement you have towards a person or situation. It may lead to stress. Judgments are not real. As a result, once you have passed judgment in your mind, negative thoughts and beliefs about a person or situation is created in you, can spoil your emotional state and relationship as well to a certain extent. We are energy, what we feel gets transferred to other person, because at the energy level we are connected.

To avoid passing judgment, it is recommended to be in the present moment and not to create any meaning out of what is being said.

If you can be a good listener who is present to someone to listen to, is great practice and it's also called serving.

If you have created a thought about a person or situation in any way. Ask yourself is it 100% true? It could be true to you but not to another person, if it is not true at global level, then it's not true, but merely your judgment.

This is the story of a girl who witnessed being judged so she decided to have her own space and comfort, where she is not being judged. She could not connect to any judgmental person.

She is determined not to be the same kind of person. She started working on herself by observing if she judges others. Because the moment you judge someone, you emanate negative energy.

Keywords – Passing judgment, the impact of judgment, Negative thinking patterns, Misconceptions and assumptions, Judgments and relationships, Emotional intelligence, Conflict resolution through understanding, Non-judgmental listening, Building better connections, being present in the moment, Mindful listening, Letting go of judgments, living without assumptions, Staying open-minded

---

Relationships are one area where you struggle the most. Improved relationships bring results in all your areas. A car has four wheels if any wheel is misaligned the car does not move. Same way in case you have bad relationship, it will impact your health, career and finances etc.

The impact of a poor relationship drains you out and you don't get the result you want in other areas of your life, because you are powerless. So, let's learn to make relationship better so that you are in resourceful state and take your life to the next level.

Chapter-12

RELATIONSHIP MASTERY

The problem in all the relationships occurs due to high expectations set by each other. If you don't meet each other's expectations, the gap begins. As a consequence, you feel alone and feel victimized, not taken care of etc.

The solution to the problem is, by reducing expectations and setting easy rules in life to be happy with each other. For example, the easy rule is, going out together for dinner not waiting to execute dinner in a five-star hotel.

Secondly, good relationships can be achieved by serving each other's values, now, if you can list down the values of your partner and your partner does the same. Once you begin serving each other's values, your relationship will go to the next level.

Below is a step-by-step guide to establish a great relationship.

- Don't let the void take place or multiply over time.
- Accept the mistakes and finish the matter and void by using simple words like "I am sorry".
- Try to return to a normal routine where you can share, chat and feel loved.
- Remember happiness is more important than being right.

- Try accepting the other partner the way they are and giving them space. Because the moment acceptance comes and resistance is dropped, the gap between two will disappear.
- There will be several things that will show the difference between the two. The behavior other partner has, may not be correct in your mind, but it may be right in his or her head.
- Choose not to pinpoint every matter or mistake, rather take the big matter only to discuss with your partner that impacts you substantially or hurts you.
- As per the reflection theory the other person is the mirror image of you. What you have inside will be reflected by the other person to you. For example, your life partner manipulates or does not give enough information to satisfy you and you don't like it. You get annoyed by his behavior. This may be your reflection coming out in front of you through him or her.

This means you have not accepted the part of you who did the same in the past or have disowned it. You hate it; hence you see the same in another person who is in front of you. In case you could forgive yourself fully and accept it. Then it will be easier for you to forgive him and accept the way a person is. It is like "What you resist persist".

Note: The above is to forgive and forget and be at peace because when you hate someone, you are still living with that person in your mind. This results in further attraction.

Very high chances are, your partner will have the traits which you have not accepted in you or someone has in your family.

Forgive and accept means not hating, showing no resistance against the person and being in peace with it.

Dropping Resistance – A lady who did not like certain traits in partner, after her study about relationship she questioned if she has resistance about personality traits in her partner towards manipulation, not being authentic etc. She came to a point and made peace with past event regarding certain personality traits towards her partner. This resulted harmony in communication.

Void of 6 Months came to an end – A story about a couple, two of them were not talking to each other for more than 6 months. A message from a lady goes to her partner asking for dinner tonight. After she realizes that there is no harm in initiating and finish the void that persisted between them. She learned in the process as if he was waiting for her to initiate it.

Her simple message brought the void to an end. They both went for dinner to the same night and showed love for each other, which brought them together once again. Later, the couple both felt, it was small action but looked very big. Soon it felt as if nothing had happened between them before. The gap of 6 months with unnecessary void was handled with one small initiative. Later the guy started making video calls to her partner every now and then. (this was due the judgement created for each other and giving more importance to ego)

Practice Balance Perspective

The problem is you think there is always problem in life. Whereas, the reality is, there is blessing in every challenge.

Balance perspective is a practice to be able to see **the blessing in disguise**. For example, you are not happy in your relationship and you find nothing exciting. There is a blessing in everything.

Let me tell you a story of girl who did not feel the connection in her relationship but due to which she could find the connection with self and could learn and grow. This would have not been possible if she could receive what she expected to experience in her relationship. She felt something is good in that situation as well.

The Practice to do: Write a list of advantages in the current relationship though current situation may not seem pleasant to you. Now also write a list of life condition that you might have if the desired expectations are met by your partner or any relationship.

Balance of Yin/Yang Energy

Another problem in the relationship begins due to a lack of understanding about the imbalance of Yin-Yang Energy. Each one of us has Yin/Yang energy. It is also called feminine and masculine energy. Every woman and man have feminine and masculine energy. Feminine Energy represents love, sacrifices, emotions & Vulnerability. The masculine energy represents being decisive, action-taking spirit, controlling etc. If it's not balanced in men or in women it becomes the obstacle in relationship as well as in career.

It has to have a blend of both energy. Anything less or imbalance will result in problems, officially and personally on both fronts. For example, a woman who has a lot of yang or masculine energy will do well financially. However, her personal life can be disturbed. Similarly, if a man has more yin will struggle in the career life and in personal life too. He will lack expression, making money, confidence and lack decision-making skills.

The solution lies in balancing the energy and being aware of the following.

- To achieve balance of yin and yang energy, you can practice affirmation, and do chakra balancing meditation along with few other actions on daily life.
- The female has to balance yin and yang by letting go of a few decisions to her partner. She has to practice vulnerability.
- Man has to make a few decisions in the house. Start with smaller ones, for Example – where to go for dinner or what to order etc.

- Men do not like to go through conflicts, so they avoid facing such situations which further pisses off the woman. If the man shows courage and stays there, it will allow his partner to vent her frustration and will dissolve by listening to her and being present.

- This is the most difficult time, when women need his man, though she may say go away, but part of her would want you to be there and hold her. She wants someone to listen to what she has to say about her emotions.

- Man has to know this fact about women that women are emotionally physical and women have to know that men are physically emotional.

- To activate famine energy women should dress well and practice self-love. And male partner has to practice the power of words by saying I am sorry, thank you, I love you. These statements will revive your relationship.

A few more common differences between males and females are as follows.

1. Emotional Expression

Females: Tend to express emotions more openly and are often better at identifying and communicating their feelings. They may focus on nurturing and emotional connection.

Males: May internalize emotions or express them through actions rather than words. They often focus on problem-solving rather than emotional sharing.

2. Communication Style

Females: Often prefer detailed, empathetic, and relationship-focused communication. They are inclined toward collaboration and connection.

Males: Tend to communicate more directly and focus on facts, outcomes, and solutions rather than emotional nuances.

3. Decision-Making

Females: Often consider emotions, relationships, and the long-term impact of decisions. They are more likely to seek input from others.

Males: Tend to focus on logic, practicality, and immediate results. They may make decisions more independently.

4. Problem-Solving Approach

Females: May approach problems holistically, considering various angles, emotions, and relationships involved.

Males: Often take a linear approach, focusing on solving the problem quickly and efficiently.

5. Risk-Taking Behavior

Females: Are generally more risk-averse, often considering safety and security before taking action.

Males: Tend to be more risk-tolerant and may take bolder actions without as much consideration for potential negative outcomes.

Let me tell you the story of a couple where a woman is not talking to her partner for a long time, due to which she finds her partner is not present to her and doesn't care about her. Based on the above guidelines and relationship counselling women opened up to her husbands, and shared what she was going through inside. Her partner remain stick to her, listen everything she had to say and apologize by saying – I am sorry, please forgive me, thank you, I love you.

All she said is, you don't have time for me. You only care about work and money. I think it is a common complaint from a woman to her man. When her partner said, he would listen to her. He loves her and kept saying continuously, she melted and hugged. In the end, she smiled because all her complaints and anger were released. The man's role is to keep looking into his wife's eyes and say – I love you, I understand my fault, I am sorry, I will take care of you from now.

Keywords – Managing relationship expectations, High expectations in relationships, Unrealistic expectations, Expectations and disappointment, Emotional gaps in relationships, Emotional intimacy, Effective communication in relationships, understanding each other's desires, reducing conflict through communication, serving each other's values, building mutual respect, Easy relationship rules, Simple ways to show love, creating happiness in relationships, small gestures in relationships, Practicing gratitude together.

Handling relationships is one skill, same as many other skills to grow holistically in life. The growth demands new learning & adopting changes etc. If you practice same what you have been from long, life will be stagnant. Hence, it is important to learn new skills or practice change, if you are willing to grow in your life. So now let's learn about the other skills you can focus on in order to grow.

Chapter-13

Significance of Developing New Skills

The problem in life comes when you are not ready to learn and change. You are born with certain skills and behavioral patterns. Later in life, you realize the need for new skills which helps you to grow and achieve goals. If you resist the new learning, you remain deprived of new experiences and new possibilities in life. What you have today, i.e. based on your present skill set, and once you upgrade your skills, you may have what you don't have currently but you wish to have.

The skills which can be developed and get you things you desire are many but few are here as examples. It should be based on your values what connect to you.

- Public speaking
- Communication skills
- Dance
- Yoga etc.
- Educator/coach
- Painter/Creative work
- Fashion
- IT Skill

These skills will help you to connect to people and bring solutions to their lives. Having new skills can open new opportunities to you.

Here is the story of a girl who left her job and decided to learn new skills to bring change in life. The first skill, she developed was to face the camera and speak in front of it. This has opened a new opportunity for her. Earlier, she learned spoken English which gave her a great career. Not only this, she could teach the language to so many people and in return she gained respect and blessings. Learning anything new just added more value and confidence in her, brought her new perspective and life.

Keywords – Embracing change, Personal development, Growth mindset, Self-improvement, Continuous learning, acquiring new skills, evolving your capabilities, breaking through limitations, overcoming reluctance to change, expanding your potential, challenging old beliefs, moving beyond comfort zones, Goal achievement through learning, unlocking new possibilities, learning to achieve your dreams, Transforming your life with skills.

Now the question comes when do we develop the new skills. Time management is concern for learning new skills, so you learn how to leverage the time now.

Chapter-14

Importance of Getting Up Early

The problem is, you don't get the idea of getting up early. At the same time, you find lack of time after finishing daily task. You question why do people get up so early. Getting up early gives you extra hours and allows you to do what you can't do, during the day. If you don't get up early you are left with a routine life to follow and at the end of the day, you carry guilt of not being able to do certain things in life.

To make sure you get up early to find those extra hours in your life, do the following:

- Make sure your why is clear to you.
- Commit to someone for some practice in the morning together.
- Plan a day in advance on an hourly basis.
- Set the alarm.
- Schedule the day from early morning till evening.
- Let yourself know if you don't get up early, and what activity you may not be able to do.

This is the story of a girl who realized getting up early, gives her extra hours in a day. Secondly, she realized this was the best time to focus on self and connect to the divine. As a Buddhist practitioner she enjoyed the morning chant so she was convinced by the idea of getting up at 4.00 am daily. Addition to it, she conducted zoom session for English-speaking classes to people who wanted to learn during lock down. Early morning hours also allowed her to do morning routines like gratitude, affirmation, visualization etc.

Keywords – Morning productivity, Early riser benefits, Extra hours in the day, The power of a morning routine, Starting the day with intention, Daily routine optimization, Maximizing your time, Overcoming procrastination. Overcoming lazy habits, taking control of your time, Setting the tone for the day, Personal discipline, creating healthy habits, building consistency, Developing accountability, Morning mindset for growth.

Now here at the end of the book, I leave you with an exercise to scale yourself and know yourself better at emotional level. So that you can decide the practice that you require to fill the gap and be happier and gain better emotional state and life.

Chapter-15

SCALING EXERCISE OF ETHICAL VALUE

I highly recommend checking your core values and emotional state. A person must analyze, an individual's behavior and emotional state so that you can work on it.

Given are few questions and answers to it will lead you to some realization.

1. Rate yourself on the percentage of negative/positive on a scale of 100. How much do you feel negative during the day and how much is positive?

   90% 10%

2. Rate yourself on a scale of 100 for the goodness you can see in others.

   80% 20%

3. Rate yourself for listening to others on a scale of 100. How good are you as a listener?

   90% 10%

4. Rate yourself on a scale of 100% for Procrastinating –
    Yes/No

    10% 90%

5. Rate yourself on a scale of 100% investing in your
    learning.

    80% 20%

6. Rate yourself on a scale of 100% contribution in some
    way in others life.

    80% 20%

The above table is furnished as an example to check the current characteristics. This activity is to be done with truthfulness. It's to know yourself and work accordingly based on guided practices.

NOTE OF GRATITUDE TO MY READERS

Thank you from the bottom of my heart for picking up this book and allowing it to be a part of your journey. This book is written with the intention of shedding light on the path to a truly happy and fulfilling life.

I am deeply grateful for your time, your trust, and your openness to embrace new perspectives. May the insights in these pages inspire you, uplift you, and empower you to create the life you desire.

Beyond my readers, I want to extend my heartfelt gratitude to my family and friends for their unwavering love and support throughout this journey. A special thank you to my **mother, brother, and sister** for always being with me emotionally, gave me strength and encouragement. And to my **wonderful husband,** who has given me the space, time, and opportunity to become the best version of myself, though I had complaints for not giving me time and importance in his life but as I believe there is blessing in disguise, today I firmly believe if he would have showered love on me, I would have never practice to seek love within. Finding love within is the highest energy to be with.

Last but not the least, thanks to my daughter who has been the biggest support, as she always trusted and encouraged to do things I wish to accomplish. Always been the support by handling herself and doing her chores herself.

Wishing you abundance, joy, and endless possibilities! ✦

With gratitude,
Diya
Pen Name (Pooja Gupta)

ABOUT THE AUTHOR

The author of the book is an Asian woman, after her MSC-Digital Marketing (Master's Degree) from Dublin, Ireland, along with 20 years of corporate experience, she got inclined to raise human consciousness. She felt human beings can be in a much more blissful state while living a daily life.

She had undergone a various training course through many spiritual masters. The field that could hold her attention is the power of the human mind and the Law of Attraction. All such teachings brought her a vivid understanding that we all have the power to heal and rewrite our destiny. The author wanted to bring what she had learned to the world through her writing.

Author's Childhood Journey

Childhood is foundation to build a character of a person and the roots of her life are formed during the childhood. Authors had a family of 8. Her childhood days were difficult as her father's business could barely provide meals for the day. Observing such a situation her mother urged her one day to give tuition when she was in 6th standard. She questioned her mother in surprise who will take tuition from a kid.

Her mother knew the family who requested to teach their children. She began teaching 3 children of her age. She was hesitant to take up this task but her mother taught that the human brain is more powerful than the body. As she grew up giving tuition, the number of students grew with time.

The school fees and education expenses were fairly managed with tuition fees. However, many times, her entire family had to sleep without a meal. Therefore, one day her mother asked her to look after her father's business. She started to give support to his father's business, along with her studies and tuition she was giving. Her involvement showed quantifiable results in business.

The family situation turned to normal and became much better. This phase was truly challenging but it taught her a few lessons. The business responsibility remained part of her life until she passed the 12th class (leaving cert).

Eventually, the institute where she completed her diploma in office management, had a hostel so she lived for a year in a hostel. Her foundation made her a strong believer in taking action. Perseverance to her became the second factor to win in life.

After completing the diploma, she joined her sister in Delhi for a job. She lacked confidence, and communication skills, however, her resolve and never giving up attitude helped her. Those days call-Centre job was very popular, so she aimed call Centre job. The level of desired communication was still missing. She practiced spoken English for a few months, and she got selected by well-known call Centre. This achievement again raised her confidence significantly.

WHAT MADE AUTHOR TO WRITE THIS BOOK

One day the idea of compiling all the learning, got infused to author's mind so she decided to write it in a diary. The learning that benefited her, became the part of her writing. During lockdown she began new practices. She did not live lock down like a curse, rather utilized the time productively.

However, soon the insecurity about not having regular income resulted in a big move in her life, she went to another country that gave pause to her writing. She focused on completing few basics in the new place, like completing master degree and getting into full time job. Gradually, she got into her normal life, then she resumed her pending writing in dark & cold nights which gave the birth to this book.

You can find me:-

Youtube: https://www.youtube.com/@LOAParadigm
Insta: Pooja_Diya_Insta
Facebook: https://www.facebook.com/profile.php?id=1124174131